THE YALE DRAMA SERIES

David Charles Horn Foundation

The Yale Drama Series is funded by the generous support of the David Charles Horn Foundation, established in 2003 by Francine Horn to honor the memory of her husband, David. In keeping with David Horn's lifetime commitment to the written word, the David Charles Horn Foundation commemorates his aspirations and achievements by supporting new initiatives in the literary and dramatic arts.

this dry spell

by keegon schuett

Foreword by Jeremy O. Harris

Yale UNIVERSITY PRESS/NEW HAVEN & LONDON

Published with assistance from the foundation established in memory of
Amasa Stone Mather of the Class of 1907, Yale College.

Yale University Press books may be purchased in quantity for
educational, business, or promotional use. For information, please e-mail
sales.press@yale.edu (U.S. office) or sales@yaleup.co.uk (U.K. office).

Set in ITC Galliard type by Integrated Publishing Solutions.
Printed and bound by CPI Group (UK) Ltd, Croydon, CR0 4YY
ISBN 978-0-300-28276-4 (paperback)

Library of Congress Control Number: 2025933940

A catalogue record for this book is available from the British Library.
Authorized Representative in the EU: Easy Access System Europe, Mustamäe
tee 50, 10621 Tallinn, Estonia, gpsr.requests@easproject.com

10 9 8 7 6 5 4 3 2 1

For inquiries regarding performance rights, please contact the author at
keegonschuett.com

Contents

Foreword, *by Jeremy O. Harris*   vii

this dry spell   1

Foreword

For the past decade language has provided safety and context for many of the most marginalized in this country, concepts that for the most cloistered or conservative among us began to feel tangible and solid. We saw ideas that had been expressed in the undercommons of queer clubs, union meetings, and playgrounds, or had fomented in the academy, spread like seeds on the wind and plant themselves into the national consciousness on CNN, *Glee*, and in the White House. Abstract concepts around "identity" blossomed and bloomed into real policies that protected the marginalized people who had first articulated them. But just as in nature, this wild new growth produced mutations, gathered weeds, and invited invasive species—leading us to the moment we are in now, where the new blossoms from the language of the past decade have come under attack before they're able to fully grow. Many just-flowering concepts are dying on the vine.

In keegon schuett's *this dry spell*, "Arizona is for everybody." Every body. Even if that body has chosen to plant itself in the ground and slowly become a cactus. What begins as a meditation on unrequited longing slowly evolves into a meditation on the limits and expanses of language. It is an arid play where, like the characters, you find yourself waiting for water, yearning for it. Water might be the static holding power of language, to fix and describe—but water also creates life in the desert. The need for language, different language, language that might flower, drives us from scene to scene with a propulsive thirst for more.

I was reminded often of Sarah Ruhl, Caryl Churchill, and Adrienne Kennedy while reading *this dry spell:* writers whose poetry is matched only by their politics. Like those writers, schuett has the uncanny ability to dissect the universal by being unflinchingly specific. Early in the play Grace, our protagonist, says, "and I don't know that there's a future. For any of us. That's why I feel kind of okay . . ." Who, this year, this month, today, has not felt this sentiment viscerally? In the case of Grace, it was in response to a would-be lover; for the rest of us, it's about everything happening around us. In a society where climate change is a fact, stasis is a recognition that the future of our species is bleak. Each of these writers found their voices in moments of immense political turmoil. There was an understanding that when the present feels like it's moving in a straight line toward a dystopian end, perhaps the way to disrupt it is through language that forges a path, one that loops back, juts jaggedly to the right before finding itself back on the left.

But what of the characters? The bodies who populate the world . . . Well there's a mother. There's always a mother. Mother May I. Mother Mary. This mother is one like few others, a sex worker who begs her child to find their orgasm. After meeting them, it's understandable how both Grace and the generations after Gen X became skeptical of sex as the determinative factor in relationships. How for many a millennial or Gen Z-er, the platonic is as important as the romantic, if not more so, much to the chagrin of the previous generation. This is the generation

of people who fast forward through sex scenes. Who lose
their virginity in their late twenties. Who fret over body
counts like Calvinists. This is counterbalanced by Grace's
Gen Alpha students who seemingly understand the world
algorithmically, through their consumption and their in-
herited fears. There's also Brahm and Jeremy, the opposing
options. The cactus and the man. And as Linda says, "I
guess some men were meant to be trees and some men will
never understand cause they think they're only meant to
cut things down."

I fear that in writing this foreword, much like our poli-
ticians and professors, language has failed me. For the
poetry that sits as the foundation of this play (a poem
inspired by a memoir written by a tortured child star) is
not at the foundation of this foreword. This play was an
oasis away from the foundation upon which I stand. Where
a fascist runs our nation and bodies like the ones at the
center of this text are under attack daily. Today, a friend
received a passport from her local passport office. She
became a flower when she was very young. Her parents
watered and celebrated her and because of all the love she
received she grew into one of the most beautiful flowers
in the world. The world took notice and took photographs
of her, put her in movies and TV shows. She became one
of the most known flowers in the world. Her license and
passport have always said she was a flower. Today my friend
received a passport from her local passport office and under
gender it didn't say F(lower) as it has since she was very
young. It said Man.

I thought of her as I read this play, and I thought of all
the productions this play will hopefully have, and I thought
of how many cacti and flowers it will save by existing.

Jeremy O. Harris

this dry spell

characters

GRACE   a tumbleweed   (early 30s, nonbinary femme)

BRAHM   a cactus   (late 20s, nonbinary masc)

LINDA   a porn star   (50s, female)

JEREMY   a really nice guy   (30s, cisgendered male)

ZUCK   a kid   (any age, any gender)

HUGH   a child   (any age, any gender)

LENT   an old soul   (any age, any gender)

note:

while the three child characters are presented as little boys
(and later, young men), casting should remain flexible on
this trio. cast inclusively and expansively.

setting:

the desert
time and space are free to blend like a sunset
pink, blue, green and everything in between

one act, 12 scenes, no intermission

1   grace and brahm kiss in the desert   p. 9

2   grace and linda on the phone   p. 20

3   grace and jeremy at an arizona public school   p. 25

4   grace and brahm decide to be "just friends"   p. 29

5   grace and linda on the phone   p. 37

6   grace teaches art to elementary students   p. 42

7   a year later, jeremy asks grace out   p. 48

8   grace visits brahm in the desert   p. 52

9   grace learns from the art class kids once more   p. 60

10   another year later, a first date with jeremy   p. 66

11   a voicemail from linda during a drug trip   p. 77

12   the world melts into a piece of art   p. 80

note:

although these scenes are divided
please consider the stage as a piece of canvas.
action should blend from scene to scene like paint.
the next scene starts as one ends.
several characters linger where they shouldn't.
grace and brahm never fully leave.
even when in other locations
it should feel like we've never left the desert.

this dry spell was developed over a weekly writing cabaret series hosted by Voices of the South, a Memphis-based theater company dedicated to new work.

The first thing shared was a poem in response to a Reedsy .com prompt about Jeanette McCurdy's memoir "*I'm Glad My Mom Died.*" Other writers listened to the poem and asked if it was a play. The rest of the play quickly arrived in the following weeks.

The play had its first reading virtually through Chicago Dramatists in the fall of 2022 with the following performers:

GRACE: Shakiera Sarai

BRAHM: Sam Sedlacek

LINDA: Alice Rainey Berry

JEREMY: Kevin Cochran

ZUCK: Christina Hernandez

HUGH: Elizabeth Archer

LENT: Jolinne Balentine-Downey

STAGE DIRECTIONS: Daniele Mathews

In the spring of 2023, the play underwent further development at Voices of the South in their physical space in Memphis, Tennessee., after a communal retreat in Snow Lake, Mississippi. The performers for this reading were:

GRACE: KT Cotten

BRAHM: Mars McKay

LINDA: Alice Rainey Berry

JEREMY: Matthew Alan Ward

ZUCK: Tracey Zerwig Ford

HUGH: Sharon Bailey

LENT: Mandy Martin

STAGE DIRECTIONS: Sharon Bailey

The 2024 reading at Yale in partnership with Long Wharf
Theatre had the following performers with direction by Brian
Fruits-Esparza and stage management by Diana Williams:

GRACE: Shakiera Sarai

BRAHM: Jaehan Pag

LINDA: Alice Rainey Berry

JEREMY: Jacob Wingfield

ZUCK: Caitlin Boho

HUGH: Megan Chan Meinero

LENT: Emily Childers

STAGE DIRECTIONS: Atlie Gilbert

"it wasn't an easy process
but that's why i did it

in life i have always been
too affable
too agreeable
too touchable
too pleasant
too wet

the one thing i did right
was eating dessert first
you get the calories you need
and the flavor you want
and a taste for what life could be

my father became a carcass
picked clean by vultures and germs
my mother became a tumbleweed
escaped this life of early birds and worms

i grew spines
not like a book
i grew needles
not like a crochet hook
i became green
and grew roots
and grew thirsty

i love it here
being baked in the sun

being caked in the dust
this waiting game for rain
is simply pure lust

never appreciated water before
always preferred a drought
not having enough feels normal
having too much feels like torture

go on
touch me now
i dare you"

—untitled poem, keegon schuett, 2022

I.

an electric, daydreamy cover of Wiegenlied Op. 49 No. 4
bellows in total darkness.
music in this world growls like a hungry animal.

distant music festival lights illuminate a couple as they make
out in the middle of the desert.
this is GRACE *and* BRAHM.

it's gentle kissing.
they pull apart.

they kiss softly again.
they stop and look at one another.
something about it is suddenly off.

GRACE   what?

BRAHM   nothing.

GRACE   no . . . what? is it me?

BRAHM   no.
it's nothing.
you've just met me at an odd time in my life.

GRACE   is that a bad thing?

BRAHM   i don't know.

GRACE   because odd isn't always bad.
sure, weird isn't always—

BRAHM   for everyone. yeah.

GRACE   but i'm not everyone either.
thank god for that.

BRAHM   are you religious?

GRACE   no, i just say "thank god"
cause it's like engrained in me. with deep roots.
same reason i say "jesus" when i'm cumming.
or sing "amazing grace" when i make someone else cum.

BRAHM   amazing grace?

GRACE   how sweet the sound!

BRAHM   you don't really—

GRACE   no.
maybe . . .
what do you think?

BRAHM   yes. maybe?

GRACE   who even has casual sex anymore?
too many risks.
too many things you can catch.

BRAHM   like herpes. the clap.

GRACE   a round of applause.

BRAHM   crabs.

GRACE   or worst of all—

BRAHM   HIV?

GRACE   no . . . feelings.
besides HIV is very treatable now.
you know that, right?

BRAHM   not from experience.
but i did see that tom hanks movie once.

GRACE   saw some friends in angels in america.
just part one.
not the sequel.

BRAHM   so we're the experts? haha.

GRACE   sure, a pair of stroikas.
but what about you?

BRAHM   what about me?

GRACE   this odd time in your life.
does that include lots of free and fun fucking?
or don't tell me. you're in a drought?
no, worse. going through a bad breakup.
never been alone before.
some girl has had you
wrapped around her finger since puberty.
you went to prom together.
fingered her at the movie theater back in 2003.
during *secret window* starring johnny depp
you threw pebbles at her secret window
with sticky buttery popcorn fingers.
that's your favorite—yellow artificial gunk.
you probably had a poster of angelina jolie

and a drawer full of crusty socks stained from your junk.
and even still, you followed this girl like a hopeful puppy.
to whatever liberal arts school she wanted to go to.
or maybe the only place she could.
no, that's it. she resented you for tailing her.
felt that you weighed her down. held her back.
reminded her of how she didn't get to go to vanderbilt.
one night, she lied to you
and fucked some random sweaty frat bro.
the lie rang in your ears like water stuck from a shower
but you stuck around cause you're a loyal golden retriever.
and finally, after years together in some boring place
like providence
she put you down and adopted a new rescue.
they are very happy together.
fade to black. credits roll. the audience leaves.
now.
here you are.
in the desert with me.

BRAHM   actually, i didn't date anyone in high school.

GRACE   oh. really?

BRAHM   not seriously anyway.
did take a girl to see *secret window* though.

GRACE   i think we all saw *secret window*.
so what's the real thing?

BRAHM   don't want to spoil a good time.

GRACE   you felt what i felt just then too . . .
didn't you?

BRAHM   i feel a lot of things.

GRACE   so then you're bi?

BRAHM   no.
i mean, i guess i am, but—
i'm just tired of feeling everything so deeply.

GRACE   maybe you're a woman.
who cares?
half the population is.

BRAHM   i'm not a woman.

GRACE   me either.
well, gender is complicated.
it's fine.

BRAHM   it's always easier to
say things like this to strangers.
isn't it?

GRACE   depends on the thing you're talking about.
familiar people turn us all into liars.
it's even at the end of the word.

BRAHM   what?

GRACE   liar. at the end of familiar.

BRAHM   oh. huh.

GRACE   cause the truth is
hard to share with the people you love.
too much at stake.
and the truth hurts.
every rose has a thorn, right?

BRAHM   most roses.

GRACE   right, sorry . . .
most roses.
then why did you come here?
not just for the music
or the dust . . .

BRAHM   no . . .

GRACE   no?

BRAHM   why did you come here?

GRACE   i asked you first.

BRAHM   and i'm asking you now.

GRACE   i came here for the music!
and the dust.

BRAHM   obviously!

GRACE   no.
really, just needed to kiss a stranger in the desert.
only that.

BRAHM   well, mission accomplished. really.
curtain call, even.

GRACE   you don't have to tell me.
that's fine too.

BRAHM   i would but—
you don't want to get involved with me.

GRACE   you ever think that—
maybe it's better for you
to not get involved with me?

BRAHM   see. i ruined it.

GRACE   it's not something you did.
it's something that just happens.
with me.

BRAHM   it's really not you.
it is me.

GRACE   isn't that a classic line?
worse than "to be or not to be."
wow.

BRAHM   "to be or not to be" isn't a breakup line.

GRACE   isn't it? in a way?

BRAHM   not the same way.

GRACE   well, all the same
this isn't the sort of thing that people do.
we don't share saliva and tangle tongues.
only for the other person to be—
tepid, inhuman—

BRAHM   inhuman?

GRACE   or some other adjective!
this isn't—

BRAHM   i know.

GRACE   actually, you don't.

BRAHM   well, actually
i know what i know.
i came here drenched in my fear of this place.

still feel like i don't know myself.
that's very scary. right?
right?!

GRACE   right!
sure.
but i don't know that—

BRAHM   right! right . . .
and i don't know that there is a future.
for any of us.
that's why i feel kind of okay . . .

GRACE   with what? abandoning one?

BRAHM   no.
that's not it.
i came here with one goal.
and it's happening.
now. that's it!

> BRAHM *digs furiously at the ground.*
> GRACE *gasps, backs away.*
>
> BRAHM *throws off their shoes.*
> *one that way. one the other.*
> *then buries their feet.*
>
> *it's really quiet out here. then—*

GRACE   oh my god.

BRAHM   yeah.

GRACE   oh my god!
i'm so sorry. i'm—

BRAHM   it's fine.

GRACE   of course, it is!
i wasn't—

BRAHM   yeah.

GRACE   i think . . . wow.
i'm so sorry.

BRAHM   i know.

GRACE   no, you don't have to.
i feel like such an asshole.
i'm so sorry.

BRAHM   no, i'm sorry.
i'm an asshole too.

GRACE   no!
you're not an asshole!
you're—

BRAHM   i don't know why i made out with you.

GRACE   you're a— you . . .
don't know why?

BRAHM   no.
i just don't know why i did.
when i know what i do.

GRACE   that . . .
you're a cactus.

BRAHM   i feel that . . .

GRACE   you're a cactus.

BRAHM   i've been
running from that knowledge every day since—well.
when you suspect that you're—

GRACE   different.

BRAHM   —a cactus.
you run from it.

GRACE   it's only natural
i suppose.

BRAHM   interesting word.

GRACE   well, it is!
we all come from the earth
we all come from nature
it makes sense that you'd want to—
it makes sense that you feel like you're—

BRAHM   it's ok.
it doesn't have to make sense to you.

GRACE   no. it makes sense to me.

BRAHM   that's ok.
it doesn't have to.

GRACE   it does!

BRAHM   ok, sorry.
i was just . . .

GRACE   i know and it's okay because i know.

BRAHM   ok. ok.

GRACE   and what now?
you're going to just stay right here?

BRAHM   yes.

GRACE   cause i sort of pictured us
walking back together.
there's still kind of a dwindling crowd . . .
somewhere over there.

BRAHM   but that's not happening now and—

GRACE   and that's ok!

BRAHM   it could have.
but it's not.

GRACE   right. well.
i'm very capable of
getting back on my own.
guess i can always
imagine something new.
i have before.

BRAHM   it was nice to have met you.

GRACE   before . . .
what did you mean by
"it could have"?

BRAHM   nothing.
it just didn't.
and that's—

GRACE   ok.
that's ok, for sure.
totally.

> GRACE *goes, but not terribly far.*
> *if there's still music, it slowly evaporates with the night.*

> BRAHM *stands firm in the harsh light of day.*

> LINDA, GRACE*'s mother, arrives on her phone.*
> *preening, applying makeup,*
> *and preparing to strip for viewers online.*

2.

LINDA   never been fond of your jokes.
could you explain it to me so i can laugh with you?
instead of at you?

GRACE   not a joke, mom.
something incredible happened
and i just want to explore it.

LINDA   what's so incredible about
being a cactus?
i've been with plenty of pricks too.

GRACE   brahm isn't— a prick.

LINDA   no, he's a cactus
and what are you, grace?

GRACE   what does that matter?

LINDA   it matters to me.

GRACE   i'm moving to arizona.
that's it. end of discussion.

LINDA   there's no end of discussion with me.
only thing that ends that is a eulogy.
i just want you to be sure of what you're becoming.

GRACE   can't i just be myself?

LINDA   oh, grace. isn't that a terribly low bar?
when i was younger
we were all told we could grow up to be anything.
a roomful of kids were all going to be
the president of the united states.
and none of us became that, but i eclipsed them all.
even still, somehow, if you can believe it
my gorgeous face isn't on any money.
i'd love to see benjamin franklin do what i've done.

GRACE   he couldn't, mom.

LINDA   no!
cause you can't store my lightning in a bottle.
and you can't soak up what i've got.
not out in a rainstorm at least!

GRACE   i know, mom, you've said.

LINDA   the point is:
i'm a damn force of nature.
and what i've done is worth more than
being on the hundred-dollar bill.
they call me a MILF now.

GRACE   i know.

LINDA   you know what that is, right?

GRACE   i do. yes.

LINDA   good, cause we all should.
everyone knows what barely legal means
but no one knows what to call
the ladies with real experience.
i mean . . . i've told you time and time again . . .
you could have what i had.
some fun experiences! maybe some even better than mine!

GRACE   mom.

LINDA   i'm only saying what i always have.
a real orgasm won't—

GRACE   enough!

LINDA   —hurt you! and pleasure won't kill you.
please listen to me when i say that!

GRACE   it's impossible to not hear you.

LINDA   i, for one
think you deserve more than a vegetable.
and if you really want one
buy yourself a cucumber and—

GRACE   don't insult my intelligence
just because i'm following my heart.

LINDA   but you're not, my love.
your heart can't think. it's no compass.

GRACE   well, that's how you feel.

LINDA   actually, it's just science.
you're smarter than this.

GRACE   maybe i'm not.
would that be okay with you?

LINDA   i need you to strive to be
a little better than this.

GRACE   i'm moving to arizona.
that's me striving toward something.

LINDA   did that cactus ask you to move there?

GRACE   no.

LINDA   what happened to the artist i knew?
you can't just uproot yourself from your own life to—

GRACE   what life?
i haven't been a real artist for a long time now.

LINDA   and when i was a little girl
i thought i would become tom cruise's new wife
and the president all in one.

GRACE   you could've been tom cruise's wife.

LINDA   that's right.
fucking nicole kidman.

GRACE   he just never met you.

LINDA   and i'm not the president either.
am i, grace?

GRACE   you could have been.

LINDA   my love, you're being delusional.

GRACE   but isn't that what all the great love songs say?
they say lose your head.
get lost in emotions.
be reckless

LINDA   and how many love songs say
kiss a cactus in the desert during a music festival?

GRACE   mom.

LINDA   how many love songs say
forget your biological clock
and grow a goddamn green thumb? tell me that, grace!
what will you get from caring for a person turned plant
in the middle of god knows where?
is getting nothing in return the kind of love you want?
do many elton john songs talk about that?
do any harry styles hits grapple with that?

GRACE   maybe more should!

LINDA   no. please.
really listen to me for once.
love isn't a hobby.
it's not just being a good kisser.
fucking—

GRACE   mom . . .

LINDA   sorry, making love, well—
it's a commitment.
you have to commit to something in order to love it.
and, for once, please commit to yourself.
love yourself.
be with someone who will actually make you cum.

LINDA   it's called kingdom come for a reason.
and GRACE

LINDA   breathe through this and find yourself.
cause it's far too early in your life
to die of thirst somewhere you don't have to.
promise me?

> GRACE *nods and puts the phone away.*
> LINDA *leaves.*
>
> JEREMY, *a man with a laptop, enters.*

3.

JEREMY   so what brings you to arizona?

GRACE   just looking for a fresh start.

JEREMY   what's wrong?
your life gone stale?

GRACE   stale, no.

JEREMY   that's a shame cause
i make a pretty great stalemate.

GRACE   what?
a stalemate is . . .

JEREMY   i know what a stalemate is.
relax. i was joking.

GRACE   oh, i didn't get it.

JEREMY   did you come here with one?

GRACE   a joke?

JEREMY   no, a stalemate.
a partner.

GRACE   no. came here by myself.
well, i came here once before and well—

JEREMY   you fell in love with it.

GRACE   yes, guess so.

JEREMY   that's the beauty of arizona.
great place for a fresh start.
lots of fresh faces.

GRACE   for sure.

JEREMY   anyway
you'll be with the kids until roughly 3:30.
the main thing is teaching the kids—

GRACE   that they can express themselves.

JEREMY   right. but you need to guide that expression.
the normal curriculum covers van gogh—
but don't mention the ear.
da vinci—
but don't ask if mona lisa is smiling or not,
warhol—

GRACE   but not his personal life?

JEREMY   no! we accept all kinds here.
why wouldn't we celebrate how he was different?

GRACE   sorry, i don't know what i was saying.
of course, you would.

JEREMY   anyhow . . .
how does all that sound to you?
can you handle that?

GRACE   yep. think so.

JEREMY   we're not looking for you
to reinvent the color wheel.
mostly just asking you to plop down in the driver's seat.
these kids don't really need art.
you're going to find that
most are already proficient in photoshop.
they don't need this. they need mandarin. but you know—

GRACE   funding.

JEREMY   right. funding.
so what did a pretty thing like you do
before moving out here?

GRACE   well, i'm not just a pretty thing.

JEREMY   it was a compliment.

GRACE   right.
well, thank you.
i got a few arts degrees and then i became a bartender.

JEREMY   bet your tolerance is wild!

GRACE   no, normal, i think.

JEREMY   bet you're a real party animal
once you put down the paint.

GRACE   no, just a normal animal like anyone else.

JEREMY   then what pulled you behind the bar?

GRACE   nothing.
i wasn't exactly lasso-ed and yanked back there.

JEREMY   right.
lasso-ed.

GRACE   lots of artists do it.
just a way to make money.

JEREMY   and get free shots.

GRACE   for some people.

JEREMY   but not you?

GRACE   i like to work with a clearer head.
but i'll say that . . .
well, i used to make the meanest mezcal margarita.

JEREMY   what's wrong with making the nicest one?

GRACE   nothing.
a mean one means . . .
another one of your jokes?

JEREMY   oh, it's fun to fuck with you.
smart to not take too many free shots.
gotta save some energy for happy hour.

GRACE   is that a thing everybody does here?

JEREMY   some of us.

GRACE   is that important? for this job?

JEREMY   just shooting my shot.
thought i could twist your arm.

GRACE   well, i'm not a pretzel.

JEREMY   then why are you so salty?
easy! i'm kidding.
just kidding around.
i've never had mezcal.
maybe you could
make your mean little drink for me sometime?

GRACE   i'm not sure that
a salty sailor like me should teach you about mezcal.
could be like teaching the kids about pollock.

JEREMY   it wouldn't be a mess like that, no.
well, you'll think about it.

GRACE   ok. i will, i guess.

JEREMY   and don't worry.
the kids will love you.

> *he closes his laptop.*
> *eats* GRACE *up with his eyes as he goes.*
> GRACE *shakes the experience off as the sun sets.*

4.

BRAHM   you actually came back.

GRACE   sure did, i—

BRAHM   you should be careful.
there are scorpions everywhere.

GRACE   what? like quicksand?

BRAHM   what?

GRACE   just that . . .
when i was small
quicksand was always a big threat.

BRAHM   this isn't like that.
there are a lot of bark scorpions around.

GRACE   is their bark worse than their bite?

BRAHM   don't be cute.
they don't bite.
they sting.

GRACE   i know that.
i wasn't being—

BRAHM   and you can't always see them.
some of them are translucent.

GRACE   translucent.

BRAHM   you can only see them
if you shine a light on them.

GRACE   really?

BRAHM   really.

GRACE   that's a lot like—

BRAHM   what?

GRACE   if a tree falls in the woods
and no one is around to see it
does it make a sound?

BRAHM   there really are scorpions.
with or without light.

GRACE   i know that.
do you think i'm in real danger?

BRAHM   aren't we always?

GRACE   no, i think there are safe places.
real ones.
maybe.

BRAHM   yeah, no.
you could be in memphis or chicago
or disney world or here.
and there's always a chance . . .

GRACE   that what?
there's a scorpion?

BRAHM   or something like it.

GRACE   i don't think that's true.
i like to think it's possible to
feel safe somewhere.

BRAHM   ok.

GRACE   you don't think a place like that exists?

BRAHM   don't know why you're asking me.
when i told you it wasn't a great idea
to get involved with me.
i meant it.

GRACE   i didn't come here just for you.

BRAHM   the music fest is over.
there's nothing out here for you.

GRACE   i just want to say that
our night together was
very important to me.

BRAHM   ok.

GRACE   and i don't exactly feel that way a lot.

BRAHM   ok.

GRACE   and don't you think—

BRAHM   what?

GRACE   that maybe . . .

BRAHM   what?

GRACE   that even as a cactus—

BRAHM   as I become myself.

GRACE   you might want more than just waiting for rain?

BRAHM   that's the plan.

GRACE   but isn't there a chance that
once you're fully a cactus you'll know something
that you don't know now?
something you couldn't have planned for—

BRAHM   it's really nice that . . .

GRACE   no, i'm sorry, i'm—

BRAHM   it's nice that
our night together was so special for you
but soon . . .

GRACE   forget soon.

BRAHM   forget what?

GRACE   soon.
i'm here now.

BRAHM   and what?

GRACE   and you're here now.

BRAHM   that night was then.
i'm becoming a cactus.

GRACE   and maybe
i'm becoming a tumbleweed!

BRAHM   you're not though.

GRACE   you don't know that.
besides! i have uprooted myself
and the wind brought me here!

BRAHM   no, you decided after we—

GRACE   well, i say that the wind brought me.
and i say that we could be
meant for each other.

BRAHM   that's nice of you
to say.

GRACE   i'm not just saying it.

BRAHM   it's romantic in theory . . .

GRACE   in real life too, i think.

BRAHM   we kissed out here. that's it.

GRACE   that's not it.

BRAHM   it is from where i'm planted.

GRACE   there's always more than
just the simple explanation.

BRAHM   not always.

GRACE   a kiss is never just a kiss—

BRAHM   it's okay to know
that some places aren't safe.
some kisses aren't—

GRACE   — a pipe is never just a pipe!

BRAHM   —fairy tale endings!
some things are as they seem.

GRACE   no, we evaded scorpion stings
but never just that—

BRAHM   it could be.

GRACE   no.
it's never just that.
cause something else will always poison you.
cupid's arrows.
or some toxic sweet sweat smell.

BRAHM   i don't sweat anymore.
it's a waste of water.

GRACE   or the story.
doing it for the story?
it's romantic fiction that's the most—

BRAHM   dangerous friction.
it's poison ivy from the first words
'til your eyes rub across the "happily ever after"—

GRACE   but those are the most beautiful stories, no?
and isn't it a waste to not savor that?
we could be one of those stories.

BRAHM   i didn't ask you to come here.
i only kissed you.
which was a mistake.

GRACE   no, it wasn't.

BRAHM   it was.

GRACE   no.
you said before i left
that we "could" have been something.

BRAHM   i don't remember saying that.

GRACE   well, i heard you.
and i felt something bigger.
you felt it too or you wouldn't have said that.

BRAHM   soon i won't say anything.

GRACE   but now you can.
you still can now . . .

> *silence*

GRACE   i'm not looking for eternal vows.
nothing like that!

BRAHM   right
and soon . . .

GRACE   that's ok. i can't promise anything either.
i'm a tumbleweed!

BRAHM   you're not.
you're not a tumbleweed.

> GRACE *approaches* BRAHM
> BRAHM *shifts away.*

BRAHM   could be scorpions on me

GRACE   i don't care.

BRAHM   but i care. this is—

GRACE   ok.
that's ok

we can take our time
and if it doesn't feel right
we can even be . . .

BRAHM   what?

GRACE   just . . . friends . . .

BRAHM   is that ok?

GRACE   of course.

> GRACE *goes.*
> *the harsh light of day returns.*

> GRACE *slowly guzzles a cup of coffee.*
> *their phone starts ringing.*

> LINDA *appears again.*
> *preparing herself for another live show.*

5.

LINDA   glad to hear the cactus is doing well.
have you two at least fucked yet?

GRACE   mom!

LINDA   what?! how do you think you got here?
it wasn't enriching conversation
or long walks on the beach.

GRACE   we're taking our time.

LINDA   no, you're running out of time.
just like me and locking down tom cruise
and becoming president.
you know i see your posts. in the middle of the night.
the lonely, raw ones.

GRACE   i delete those.

LINDA   i'm awake a lot later than you think.

GRACE   ok.

LINDA   i've got onlyfans subscribers up
all over the world.
literally!

GRACE   ok, mom!

LINDA   listen, everything starts young.
especially doubt. and you're still young!
i could've given you up
but my mother would've never allowed it—

GRACE   i'm not full of doubt—

LINDA   —and i'm glad i didn't get rid of you!
now, at least.

GRACE   that's awfully comforting.

LINDA   what?
am i s'posed to coddle you with cozy lies?!
life is about cold truths.

GRACE   not always.
you could say something warm.
wouldn't burn the world to a crisp.

LINDA   well, settling down with a cactus is a mistake.

GRACE   so you've said.

LINDA   you're so young!
you have to start your best life as soon as possible.
it's the tortoise and the hare.

GRACE   that story is about taking your time.

LINDA   no, it's about losers winning for once.

GRACE   so i'm a loser to you.

LINDA   grace, even tortoises . . .
torti? . . . tortoises . . . ?
jesus!
even fancy turtles fuck.

GRACE   ok! i hear you!
loud and clear!

LINDA   but you don't listen.

GRACE   i do! constantly.

LINDA   everything is ticking away inside of you
like some kind of *die hard* bomb.

GRACE   and you would know
you were in the *die hard* parody in 1989.

LINDA   *die hard-on.*
yeah, i've been with sweaty clowns with big dicks
imitating stars i've never met.

GRACE   you've been with actors.

LINDA   that doesn't make what we had
into something false, my love!
i never got to marry bruce willis either.

GRACE   but you could've.

LINDA   fucking demi moore.

silence

LINDA   i can't help this pull in me.
i have the tide and gravity
and fuckin' salvador dali alarm clocks in my rib cage
asking for you to . . .

GRACE   what? do more than i am?

LINDA   yes, my love.
i just don't want you to wake up one day—

GRACE   i'm not asleep.

LINDA   —and realize you could've been living life.

GRACE   wow.

LINDA   instead of acting out some sort of—

GRACE   what?

LINDA   —bedtime story.
some sort of fairy tale.
this thing with the cactus is—

GRACE   none of your business.

LINDA   actually, fantasies are my business.

GRACE   no, mom.
selling your body is your business.

LINDA   i don't know how i raised such a prude!

GRACE   cause you didn't!
grandma did.
while you had all your fun.

LINDA   got it.
i'm a monster.
you love the plant but hate my implants.

GRACE   no! you're allowed to do what you want
with your body . . .

LINDA   oh, thank you! thank god—!

GRACE   but i am too!

LINDA   —amazing grace! how sweet the sound!

GRACE   just . . .
could you back off a bit?
please?

LINDA   i'm open-minded, grace. i really am.
i've done everything under the sun twice
just to be sure i wasn't missing anything.
hate me all you want
but if you're not going to touch his thorns
could you at least get some shears and cut away at yours?

GRACE   we're taking our time.

LINDA   well, don't take forever.
that's a real long time.
and you deserve to have a real orgasm. soon!

> *as the call ends,* GRACE *enters a classroom.*
> *three children,* ZUCK, HUGH, *and* LENT, *also enter*

> *they aggressively scribble on blank sheets of paper before . . .*

6.

ZUCK   mrs. arbor . . .

GRACE   i'm not married.
please call me mx. arbor.

HUGH   like trail mix?

GRACE   exactly like that.

HUGH   like nuts, huh?

LENT   how come you ain't married yet?

GRACE   we're not here to talk about that.
we're here to create something special.
so please focus on your paint and—

ZUCK   my momma says
marriage is about creating something special though.

HUGH   ain't marriage a type of art, mx. arbor?

GRACE   to some. but today we're making artwork.

LENT   my momma and daddy made it work.
they did yessir and they made me.
i'm something special, right?

GRACE   sure. now if you blend yellow and blue
you'll find that—

ZUCK   i'm not looking to find much in this life.
my momma says to me
to be careful of guns
when i get on the bus
cause i could die, cause of guns.

HUGH   you have a gun, miss arbor?

LENT   mx. arbor!

ZUCK   oh yeah, that's right.
you gotta gun, mx. arbor?
or are you just out in these streets
real brave and stuff? just on yer own?

GRACE   i don't have a gun.

HUGH   are we even safe here then?

LENT   what're you gonna do?
if something happens?

ZUCK   and something always happens!

HUGH   when you least expect it

LENT   which is always

ZUCK   all the time

GRACE   let's forget that!
let's MIX it up and focus.
remember we're depicting our homes.
just drawing where we live.
what are you working on, lent?

LENT   my house
like i'm sposed to!

GRACE   ok. tell me about it.

LENT   i will.
but whydontyou
tell me about your boyfriend first?

GRACE   don't have one of those.

LENT   so you've got a girlfriend then!
what's she like?

GRACE   i like the way you've done the roof.
that'll keep out the rain.

LENT   it don't rain here much.
did it rain where you're from?

GRACE   no, it snowed.

LENT   that's too bad.
my condolences.

ZUCK   condolences is . . .
a funeral type thing to say.

LENT   well, snow is like the funeral of weather, stupid.

ZUCK   don't call me stupid!

LENT   but you are.

ZUCK   i ain't.

LENT   but you are

ZUCK   i really ain't

HUGH   whoa whoa!
he ain't, man, that's not cool!

LENT   nothing's cool. know why?
the planet's gonna heat up with us on it
and we're gonna just evaporate one day.
don't matter if she's got a girlfriend or a boyfriend
don't matter if she's a mrs. or somethin' else.
the world is gonna flood like noah and the ark.

HUGH   just like noah and the ark!

GRACE   calm down!

LENT   no!
the whole wide world is ending
just like i saw in *veggietales!*

HUGH   just like *veggietales!*!

LENT   i don't eat vegetables because they're holy.
they're god's friends.
they wrote the bible.

ZUCK   some people eat cucumbers.

HUGH   and that's a sin.

LENT   uh huh! that's right.

GRACE   enough! that's enough!
the assignment was "where i'm from."
we're painting our homes.
what do you have over here?

ZUCK   this is a realistic rendering of my mother's uterus.
yup. that's where i'm from.
i was there for ten months
and then somebody cut me out.
guess you could call me a refugee of sorts.

GRACE   no . . . that's not—

HUGH   well, hey! mx. arbor!
look at mine.
mine is an abstract representation of where my folks live.
even got the cactus out front.
it's real prickly.

LENT   could hurt ya

HUGH   could hurt ya real bad

GRACE   well, a cactus is just a plant . . .

ZUCK   well, yeah.

HUGH   we know that.

LENT   ohhhhh . . .

ZUCK   ooooooo . . . !
she's in love with a plant!!

HUGH   she's gotta green thumb!!!

ZUCK   ooooooooOOOooooooooooOOOoooooo!!!!!
HUGH
and LENT

LENT   mx. arbor and a cactus sitting in a tree . . .

GRACE   that's enough.

ZUCK   k i s s e n g!
HUGH
and LENT

GRACE   i n g.

ZUCK   what?

GRACE   if you're going to make fun of me
you better get the spelling right.

ZUCK   why?

HUGH   yeah why?

ZUCK   we got autocorrect, don't we?

LENT   is there really a point to any of this?

GRACE   i don't know, kids.
probably.

> *the kids fold up their masterpieces and wander off.*

> *the desert vibrates with the classic lullaby tune.*

> BRAHM *grows spines from his arms.*
> GRACE *keeps their distance.*

another year gone.
GRACE *sighs.*

JEREMY *approaches with just his satchel.*

7.

JEREMY   how was your first year here, party animal?

GRACE   oh, fine.

JEREMY   fine?

GRACE   actually bad.
it's been horrible.

JEREMY   gathered that on my own.
normally more of a hunter than a gatherer
but here we are.

GRACE   i shouldn't have come here.

JEREMY   no. arizona is for everybody.
even party animals like you.

GRACE   i'm not a—

JEREMY   the heat isn't for everyone
especially old people
but that's another story.

GRACE   what's up, jeremy?

JEREMY   i got a number of calls that said—

GRACE   what?

JEREMY   well, that you're dating a plant.
that true?

GRACE   i didn't tell the kids that—

JEREMY   but the kids told their parents that.
so . . . ?

GRACE   i have a friend who is
becoming a cactus.

JEREMY   right on. that's cool.
i think cactuses are sick. sick—cool!
not sick—like mentally ill.
but even if they were they're still
uh, neat!

GRACE   neat. right.
well . . . thanks for understanding.

JEREMY   and you're not dating the cactus?

GRACE   it's complicated.

JEREMY   everything is, isn't it?
i nearly failed algebra two
but my mom emailed the teacher
and begged for me to get a d.
you ever get a d in anything?

GRACE   not that i can remember.

JEREMY   you want to?

an absolutely wild silence

JEREMY   haha! just kidding.
i'm only saying that as a joke.
i completed the sexual harassment booklet.

GRACE   me too.

JEREMY   and i was just asking if
you got a d in a class ever . . .
and then i said . . .
well, i tried to tell a joke.
you didn't laugh so—
maybe i offended you.

GRACE   you didn't.
it's like all of your jokes—
it's ok, jeremy.

JEREMY   oh, thank god.
or thank goodness!

GRACE   yes . . .
thank goodness.

JEREMY   to be clear—
i don't really care what you do in your personal time—

GRACE   that's good.

JEREMY   but that is, unless if . . .
well . . . if you have time . . .

GRACE   are you asking me out?

JEREMY   i am asking if—
you'd be open to hanging out outside of work and
just seeing what's up with all of that.

GRACE   i don't know.
still sort of new around here.

JEREMY   it's been a whole year, grace.
and the desert can get real cold at night, you know?

GRACE   yes. i know.

JEREMY   well, i know
some hot spots around town is all i'm sayin
cool places you could stay warm at.

GRACE   i'll think about it, jeremy.
is that ok?

JEREMY   of course!
but next year . . .
it might be best if you don't mention your cactus friend.
not to the kids.
i think it's cool
but they barely know how to spell their own names
so it'll just confuse them.
you understand?
so i'll pick you up at seven some friday?
this friday? maybe next? maybe two from now?
i'm a hunter not a gatherer.

he leaves.

GRACE *returns to the heart of the desert.*
BRAHM *seems so much more like a cactus now.*

it's quiet between them.

8.

BRAHM   haven't you had enough
of this?

GRACE   maybe i'm a glutton for punishment.

BRAHM   that's exactly what i mean.
if it's punishment.

GRACE   most things are
but not this.

BRAHM   shouldn't you go somewhere else?
find someone else to kiss in the desert?

GRACE   maybe i will.
one day.

BRAHM   it's concern that makes me say it.

GRACE   well, don't be concerned about me.
i can take care of myself.

BRAHM   that's good.
cause i'm not sure this part of me will exist much longer.

GRACE   right.
i've been meaning to ask—
does your family know you're—
do they know that you're—

BRAHM   they know what's important.

GRACE   if they're like my mom, i'd bet—

BRAHM   what's she like?
your mother . . .

GRACE   well!
linda's very comfortable in her body.
and so is everyone else!

BRAHM   what does that mean?

GRACE   nothing. it's stupid.
she does porn.

BRAHM   oh. that's interesting.

GRACE   is it? it's just sex.
and not even real sex.
it's all performance.
and faking it.
i do admire how free she is—

BRAHM   with her body?

GRACE   no
her words.
i mean i love her and
i guess, she means well—

BRAHM   but?

GRACE   she picks at me like i'm a scab.
constantly wondering what i'm going to do next.
the art i'll make, the love i'll make.
she looks at me like i'm some freak version of her.
who can't figure out that my body is my friend.
and not my prison.

BRAHM   i understand that.

GRACE   i don't know how to explain it to her.
that i'm not sick.
there's nothing to heal here.
it makes it hard to talk to her.

BRAHM   it was hard to tell my parents
about coming here

GRACE   my mom told me i was throwing my life away
and i said "what life?"

                              they laugh together for a moment.

BRAHM   before this, i knew music.
and that's enough for a life.

GRACE   you knew music?

BRAHM   felt like i had a drumset in me.
not a heart really.
kept feeling that rhythm of "badumtiss."
the punchline after jokes.
it's hard to have the feeling of comedy inside you
that feeling of being the butt of the joke . . .

GRACE   but the butt is the penthouse of the legs.

BRAHM   that's not funny.
after what i said that's not—

GRACE   i'm sorry.
guess it doesn't really matter if your folks know.

BRAHM   my folks? haha.

GRACE   yes, haha!
maybe a weird word to use but—

Scene 8 55

BRAHM   but everything feels weird these days.
it feels like a million years ago
when they sat me at a piano
to tickle keys.
then one day you realize you're not unlocking anything.
and i loved making music.
but it always felt like
my parents had an idea for me.
it's this rhythm
they want you to—

GRACE   continue.

BRAHM   right
but things have changed
music doesn't sound the same.

GRACE   i get that.
i used to feel tethered to something
when i could hover over a canvas.
feels like i lost that feeling somewhere.
i don't want to paint anymore.
and i've spent so much of my life
wanting to paint.

BRAHM   what changed?

GRACE   maybe i have.
there's something embarrassing about
trying to create something beautiful.
when you feel ugly all the time.

BRAHM   but you're not ugly.

GRACE   i'm not looking for safe words right now.
can you be real with me too?

BRAHM   of course.

GRACE   when we met, you said that
i met you at a strange time in your life.

BRAHM   yes?

GRACE   i think that's true of me too.

BRAHM   but maybe
every part of life is a strange time.
it would be weird to operate as if this wasn't
all happening to us for the first time.

GRACE   some people do!
some people look at a calendar
and know where they're supposed to be.
next april, i won't be a fool.
next july, we send out that promotion.

BRAHM   by the time i'm forty,
i'll have x, y, and z figured out.

GRACE   and here you are.
sometimes i think you're the one who has it all figured out.

BRAHM   i don't but—
these days, scorpions are definitely on me.

GRACE   really?!

BRAHM   and yesterday, hummingbirds came by.
one day, hummingbirds will feed from me
all the time.

GRACE   wow. that's beautiful
don't you think?

BRAHM   i only think about water now.
water and hummingbirds and dust
and water . . .

GRACE   only all of that?

BRAHM   ashes to ashes
dust to dust
hummingbirds to hummingbirds

GRACE   can i ask if—
do you remember seeing me?

BRAHM   from just now?

GRACE   from before.
at the festival.
you remember that?

BRAHM   yeah.

GRACE   does the memory flutter in you?
like a hummingbird?

BRAHM   in a way, maybe.
but it's hard to describe
because hummingbirds feel different now.
my heart feels different now.
skin feels dryer now.
and i don't cry anymore.

GRACE   did you cry a lot before?

BRAHM   it's not important.

GRACE   it is to me.
might be to your—

BRAHM   never mind that.
when i saw you then . . .
things were everything that they're not now.
it doesn't make sense.
our eyes got stuck to each other.

GRACE   like velcro.

BRAHM   right, vel– veeta.
and now i struggle to find them at all.
i am a little afraid that—
no, never mind.

GRACE   no, what?
you can tell me.

BRAHM   i know.

GRACE   i feel like i could tell you anything.

BRAHM   i know.

GRACE   and that makes me feel nutty
but i like that about being with you.

BRAHM   i know.

GRACE   so you can tell me.
you don't have to but—

BRAHM   and what if i don't want to.
is that okay?

GRACE   of course!

BRAHM   cause sometimes
it feels like i have to.

GRACE   you don't have to.
we don't have to tell each other everything.
that's not what . . . this is.

BRAHM   you wanted to say love?

GRACE   too soon to say that, isn't it?
it's only been a year.

BRAHM   that long already?
felt like an hour to me.

GRACE   only an hour?

BRAHM   a lot can happen in an hour.

GRACE   right.

BRAHM   even more can happen in a minute.
all depends, doesn't it?

GRACE   yes.

BRAHM   a lot of paint can dry in an hour.
you could make a lot in that time.

GRACE   that's a beautiful thought.

BRAHM   and you should be able to do it.
since you don't believe in dangerous places.

> *in the silence, the children return.*

> *they unfold their masterpieces from before.*
> *they splatter paint on the pages furiously.*

> GRACE *stands in awe until—*

9.

ZUCK   did you want to be a teacher
when you were our age?

GRACE   maybe.

HUGH   "maybe" ain't a real answer.

LENT   to some people it is.

GRACE   correct.
do you want to be a teacher?
is that what you're drawing?

ZUCK   no, i'm drawing conclusions.
i look around
and i see that y'all say it gets cold and snows at christmas.
but here? never has.
it might get cold at night but it's hotter than hell during
the day.

HUGH   hotter than hell, yessir!

ZUCK   and i been told that it's santa
who brings the presents,
all in a big ol' sleigh with reindeer.
just flyin' through the sky.
but i know deer and i know they're just
levitatin' in front of a plane
staring blankly at it.

LENT   they're always in the way, huh?

HUGH   with cars and such.

GRACE   so you want to be a pilot? or . . . ?
do you want to be santa?

ZUCK   no.

HUGH   santa claus ain't real, mx. arbor.

LENT   grace, you still believe in santa claus?

GRACE   please don't call me—

ZUCK   grace's old enough to know that he's just an idea.

HUGH   and not all ideas are real.

LENT   some things are
bedtime stories.

ZUCK   or myth.

HUGH   or rom coms.

LENT   or scripture.

ZUCK   mmhmm.

GRACE   please call me, mx. arbor.
don't use my first name.

ZUCK   oh, i'm sorry.
i gotta mom and a dad
and my dad has a casey.
you're kinda like a casey away from home to me.

HUGH   my mom has a casey too!

ZUCK   it would feel weird
to call em mister
or missus

HUGH   or mx

ZUCK   cause they're just casey's

HUGH   and casey's are all over.
your parents still together?

LENT   yep. but they need to give up on that dream.
they're bad for each other.
it's just that the sex is too good.

ZUCK   oh. that can happen.
sex is a good way to erase problems.

HUGH   can be. for a bit

LENT   for a bit. sure.

GRACE   aren't those presents?

ZUCK   sure are, mx. arbor.

GRACE   and you don't want to be santa claus?

ZUCK   no, see
i think one day i'll be the real santa
which is all those people in the cars
with the boxes and plastic bags.

HUGH   oh! an amazon person!

LENT   wonder woman was an amazon.
she's a heroine.

ZUCK   heroin is a drug. amazons are different.
they're the ones who really bring stuff.

HUGH   but soon that'll be just robots.
lil' drones.

LENT   drones?

HUGH   they're like little helicopters
that brings your stuff.
see, mx. arbor, i drew one.
i want to fly drones.

ZUCK   those are used for war!

HUGH   everything's fair in love and war
and everything useful gets used in both.

GRACE   where did you hear that?

HUGH   tiktok.

LENT   she didn't want to be a teacher.
i get that.
who does?
i'm here to learn.
the world is all about learning.

GRACE   it is.

LENT   and you're only here to learn from us, ain't you?

ZUCK   those who can't do, teach, right?

GRACE   that's an ugly thing to say.

ZUCK   well, it's an ugly world, mx. arbor.
we can't all be roses and daisies
and mistletoes wigglin' from the ceiling.
sometimes you gotta look around
and see that we live on a pimple.

HUGH   gonna pop one day.

ZUCK   and when it does, i'll be an amazon person.

HUGH   i'll be a drone flyer person. for war or love or
whatever.

LENT   and i plan on just learning all i can
which is really just a teeny tiny portion
of all human knowledge.
i will read the books i can.
i'll watch the films i can.
i'll listen to the music i can.
i'll be every kind of person i can be.
i'll be good. i'll be bad.
i'll be healthy. i'll be sick.
i'll be helpful. i'll be selfish.
i will see the world
and i will never use a mirror for too long.

ZUCK   i think i'm gonna stay the same my whole life.

HUGH   that's one way to do it.

ZUCK   yessir that's one way to do it!

GRACE   you don't want that.

ZUCK   but i do. i'm fine just that way i am.

GRACE   no. you're going to change.
i didn't always want to be a teacher.
when i was little
i thought deeply about becoming a veterinarian.

LENT   you wanted to put cats and dogs to sleep?

GRACE   no! i wanted to heal them.

LENT   but ain't death a big part of it?
like just killing them when stuff gets hard?

GRACE   everything gets hard.
and i didn't become a veterinarian.

ZUCK   so then you became a teacher.
what exactly are you healing here?

LENT   that's the wrong question.

HUGH   yeah?

LENT   question is . . .
what's she putting to sleep here?

ZUCK   grace. sorry, mx. arbor!
ain't doing that. i can tell.

LENT   no. you can't always tell. she can't tell.
nobody wants to learn and nobody wants to teach.
everybody's a leech. everywhere is getting drained.
nothing has roots anymore.
nothing!

GRACE   let's take a deep breath
and move on.
in fact, let's take some red and some blue—

LENT   and what?
make purple? grow up.

> *the children fold up their works of art and go.*
> *the familiar lullaby music swells again.*

> BRAHM *is now very much a cactus.*
> *only small traces of human remain on his face.*

> *another year has slipped away.*
> GRACE *sighs as it goes.*

> JEREMY *returns. thirsty and hungry.*
> *laughing drunkenly in that fun first date way*

10.

JEREMY   not exactly my kind of music
but thanks for finally coming out with me.

GRACE   you're welcome.
only took you two years to convince me.

JEREMY   two years with the kids helped.

GRACE   helped what exactly?

JEREMY   wear you down, maybe.
a few more years
and you'll get the hang of it.

GRACE   sure.
like someone in the gallows.

JEREMY   it is rough.
i get it.
but kids'll do that to you.

GRACE   they're all about pressing buttons.

JEREMY   lately, it's more like scrolling or swiping
but they'll find the tender part of you
and pinch it. pull at it.

GRACE   i'm not afraid of being challenged.
just don't like it.

JEREMY   who does? that's just what kids do.
they don't know any better

GRACE   they do. they're just rude.

JEREMY   no, they come into the world that way
and say "wow! what a mess you've made of the place!"
then we tell them to clean their rooms until they accept that—
yeah, basically everything is a mess
and they've got to own their part in it.
their diapers get added to the pile too.

GRACE   they know more than you think.

JEREMY   is that so?

GRACE   listen, i don't want to have kids.

JEREMY   oh. ok?

GRACE   sorry. i just feel like that's—
maybe i should say that now

JEREMY   i think it's a responsible thing to say. i do.
that being said . . . time changes all of us.
nobody wants to stay the same forever

GRACE   nobody. you sure about that?

JEREMY   i'm not sure of anything these days.

GRACE   do you want to have kids?
or are you like me?

JEREMY   i think i'm like you.

GRACE   really?

JEREMY   but i don't know.
for one, i want money.
everyone with kids seems like
they're telling you why they're okay
with not having money.
or saying things like:
"you couldn't possibly understand the feeling!"

GRACE   couldn't possibly!

JEREMY   it feels like a magic trick.

GRACE   yes!

JEREMY   like when people tell you
to move to new york city.
some people have fun there, but . . .

GRACE   but?

JEREMY   it feels like a trap.

GRACE   yes
but everything is in its own way.

JEREMY   my couch is a trap.
might as well have claws coming out of it.
holding me in place.

GRACE   my phone is a trap.
my eyes get stuck to it like glue.
like a little wiggling mouse.

JEREMY   my email is a trap.

GRACE   oh, that's a good one!

JEREMY   like a net dropped into the ocean . . .

GRACE   and when you pull it up, it's what?

JEREMY   just empty cans and cans . . .

GRACE   of spam?

JEREMY   yeah! licked clean by future sashimi.

GRACE   i read somewhere
that we're running out of healthy fish.

JEREMY   now see, i heard
there's plenty of fish in the sea.
plenty means lots.

GRACE   right, but i said healthy.

JEREMY   right, and you're a healthy fish?
you're one of the healthy ones?

GRACE   you're funny in your way, jeremy.

JEREMY   but what?

GRACE   i'm not a fish.

JEREMY   i didn't say you were a fish.
but maybe you're a mermaid!

GRACE   not that either.
besides mermaids were just manatees.

JEREMY   what?

GRACE   would you call me a manatee?
right to my pretty-thing party-animal face?

JEREMY   no, never.
i just never heard that—

GRACE   well
that's what columbus lusted over.

JEREMY   manatees?

GRACE   yes.
when he came to the "new world."

JEREMY   wow.
well, men go crazy at sea.
that's a thing.

GRACE   men go crazy on land, too.

JEREMY   that's true! that's real.
i wasn't saying you were a fish.

i'm sorry.
didn't mean that the way it sounded.

GRACE   then how did you mean it?

JEREMY   i don't know.
salmon swim upstream to where they were born
and then they die.

GRACE   what's that supposed to mean?
for you and me?

JEREMY   when i chase after an idea in my own head,
i wonder if it's evolved or if it's gasping for the first time.
my ideas just might be used to saltwater. i dunno.
there's something about you.
something about the way you hold yourself.
makes me want to chase you.
you're just like a living question mark.

GRACE   in what way?

JEREMY   see!
a question mark would ask that.
an exclamation point would slap me.

GRACE   oh wow!
well . . . if anything
i'm a comma.

JEREMY   how's that?

GRACE   i dunno . . . i feel this way when i paint.
things blend.
always feel like i'm
breaking up my ideas with little breaths.

i like the idea of things going on
and on and on
you say an idea
then think

JEREMY   and say one more?

GRACE   yes, cause life is a run-on sentence.
someone will tell you it's wrong
try to stop you somewhere.

JEREMY   but there's no final place?

GRACE   something is continuing
and it's coming from me somehow
i'm just a part of a fragment
and i'm just there giving space for you to breathe
your lungs fill, then they release
and i'm part of that release

JEREMY   and you feel this when you paint . . . ?

GRACE   right.
i get to be part of the moment when
pink somehow becomes blue.
that make sense?

JEREMY   sure. i think so.
and i think i'm a colon
but only cause i'm always talkin' shit.

GRACE   that's so stupid.
and you're more like a semicolon.

JEREMY   what? like i'm half-assing this date?

GRACE   no. you're like every other semi-colon.
don't know where to put you yet.
do you have an official place?

JEREMY   ohhh . . .
but i'll figure out where to put myself.
i'm good at that.
if you don't mind.

GRACE   no . . .
guess i don't.

JEREMY   when i met you
you mentioned the meanest mezcal margarita.
but i didn't know what mezcal was.

GRACE   oh my god.
that was forever ago.

JEREMY   it was only two years ago.

GRACE   mezcal.
well, it's like tequila but—

JEREMY   no, i know what it is now.
you don't have to tell me.
i have google too.

GRACE   oh, ok . . .

JEREMY   i tried to search for it. to try it.
it's becoming more popular, i guess.

GRACE   sure.

JEREMY   it's an art form. mezcal.
they bury the agave and burn it.

feels funereal in a way.
and then the waiting
for the flavors to come together. all that smoke. ascension.

GRACE   right.

JEREMY   autocorrect thought i was looking
for mescaline.
you know what that is?

GRACE   not intimately.

JEREMY   interesting choice of words!
for a woman who fell in love with a cactus.

GRACE   excuse me?

JEREMY   it comes from cactuses!

GRACE   but i'm not a woman.

JEREMY   right, well—
i can't give apologies out for everything.

GRACE   i'm not asking you to.
but you could say—

JEREMY   if you spend your whole life apologizing,
you'll never say something exciting.

GRACE   i don't think that's true.

JEREMY   you ever heard an exciting apology?
didn't think so.

GRACE   fine.
then tell me . . .

what is mescaline?
since i couldn't possibly know.

JEREMY   depends.
some think it's a drug.
some say medicine.
your friend might think it's something else

GRACE   my friend?

JEREMY   it comes from cactuses.

GRACE   cacti . . .

JEREMY   so i thought you'd be familiar!

GRACE   familiar people turn us all into liars.

JEREMY   cactuses, cacti
same difference.
anyway, i got some!
don't tell your little friend . . .

GRACE   mescaline?

JEREMY   thought maybe
we could try it together.

> *he produces a travel coffee container*
> *and two red plastic cups from his satchel.*

GRACE   i'm sorry, but no.
i don't really do drugs anymore.

JEREMY   but like i just said
it's medicine!

GRACE   to some people.

JEREMY   and it's made from cactuses.

GRACE   cacti . . .

JEREMY   cacti! exactly!
might help you
see from your third eye
which maybe will give you a clearer view than
the two you've got.
listen, you don't have to drink it with me
but we're already a little tipsy
and i thought we could tip further over.
like the titanic. i thought you'd like this idea!

>   *he pours from the coffee container into one plastic cup.*
>   *gently urges* GRACE *to take it.*

>   *they don't.*

JEREMY   c'mon! could be good for you.
i'm hoping it'd be good for me too.
maybe some cactus juice can help me too.

>   *he downs that cup and pours another.*
>   *he extends it to* GRACE *again.*

JEREMY   and maybe you'll trust me enough
to introduce me
to your little friend.
i'd like that.
never met a cactus.
not one like him anyway.

GRACE   never?

JEREMY   not while i'm high on cactus juice!

GRACE   i met brahm out here.

JEREMY   then he's close by?

GRACE   somewhere out here.

> GRACE *takes the cup.*

JEREMY   i thought you were a comma.
and commas connect ideas, right?
isn't that what you do?
or are you in a coma, sleeping beauty?

> GRACE *drinks it.*

GRACE   i'm not in a coma

> *a lot of time passes, quickly.*
> *glowing scorpions scatter.*
> *stars move across the sky.*

> LINDA *appears like morning dew*
> *as* GRACE *and* JEREMY *get high.*
> *doing her makeup carefully, slowly.*

II.

LINDA   my chosen name means pretty.
of course, some people thought i copied linda lovelace
but my name is my own.
and i'm a lot deeper than just my throat.
my words come from somewhere else.

somewhere lower.
i went by linda like cher.
just linda.
i believed that i was pretty above all else.
cause i was.
just linda.

there's something insane about going to the grocery store
and being another one of the pieces of meat
that men consider.
they're making dinner, sure
but they make eyes too.

isn't it fun? that phrase?
make eyes?
like something you have as an appetizer.
you make eyes and then you make conversation
and finally, you have dessert.
you make love.
i always eat dessert first.
while i still have room for it.

plenty of men have made love to me.
but the truth is
i'm the one who made it love.
i don't know what they were making for themselves.

they're really just boys.
burning ants under magnifying glasses.
is that making eyes too?

i made all that fucking into something sweet.
something chocolate.
something shimmering in sprinkles.
something caramel
with whipped cream.

with strawberries
sucked in.
gulped down.
savored.
cause you can't taste life by only making eyes.
seeing things isn't the same as loving them.
you have to have room to love things properly.

doesn't matter if you're nicole kidman
or demi moore
or linda lovelace
or even just yourself.

you have to have dessert sometime.
have it first sometimes.
you deserve it and you should know that.

sooooo . . .
call me back when you get this.
please call me back.
i'm sorry for everything i've said.
especially the true things.

it's your life.
you're allowed to screw things up the way you want to.
i believe that. i really do.
i love you.

> *she strokes their faces and feels* BRAHM*'s skin.*
> *then she moves with the stars and the scorpions.*

> *she disappears.*

> JEREMY *stands before* BRAHM.

12.

JEREMY   have you ever really
touched his skin?

GRACE   i have.

JEREMY   can you call it that . . .
when it's a plant?
would you say husk instead?

GRACE   does it matter?

JEREMY   yes.
it matters what things are called.
and that should be very important to you
as a teacher.

GRACE   well, it's not.
i'm only an art teacher.
an elementary school art teacher. god.
most of my paintings don't even have names.

JEREMY   but they should!
imagine this place if it didn't have a name . . .
how could you tell people about it?

GRACE   this place doesn't have a name.
and i think i could.

BRAHM   not everything needs to have the same name
to everyone.

JEREMY   it still talks!
do you remember your name?
you remember the alphabet?

GRACE   does it matter?
does it make a real difference?

JEREMY   i think so.
if i was a cactus—

BRAHM   but you're not.

JEREMY   i'd want to remember things.
some things.
i'd want to at least be able to remember . . .

BRAHM   the name of arizona.

GRACE   did you want to touch him?
is that why you asked?
about his skin?

JEREMY   no . . . i was just curious.
if he was spiky yet?

GRACE   what does it look like?

JEREMY   he looks spiky.
but he could be soft
like it could just be . . .

GRACE   what?
like hair gel?

JEREMY   yeah like some kind of
there's something about mary hair gel.
no harm in that.
just something that washes off of you.

GRACE   i don't know why you think
my paintings need names.

JEREMY   everything deserves to be named!

GRACE   deserves makes it sound like a punishment.

JEREMY   that's a weird way to hear what i said.

GRACE   and what?
should i apologize for hearing it the way i heard it?

JEREMY   no.

GRACE   want to hear another
classically boring apology?!

JEREMY   of course not.

GRACE   defining a painting robs it of
its mystery . . .

JEREMY   ok.

GRACE   and this world needs some mystery.

JEREMY   does it?

GRACE   yes! otherwise . . .
we're all just getting boxed into job titles or relationships
or adjectives that don't actually describe us!
drawing things the same way they've always been drawn.

JEREMY   ok.
i was just trying to ask
if his skin could hurt you.
wasn't trying to start a fight.

BRAHM   you can touch me.
if you want to feel for yourself.

JEREMY   really?
is that ok?

> *he approaches* BRAHM *slowly*
> *hands out*
> *like approaching a horse that could kick your head off*

GRACE   you should be careful.

JEREMY   why?
you think i'm gonna fall in love with him too?

GRACE   no.

JEREMY   i'm not going to fall in love with a cactus.
that's ridiculous.

GRACE   because of the scorpions.
there are bark scorpions on him
and their sting is worse than their name.

JEREMY   those are only really dangerous
if you're a child.

GRACE   then maybe i am one.

JEREMY   why?

GRACE   cause i'm afraid.

JEREMY   of bark scorpions?
are you really afraid of little bugs?
they're basically just bumblebees
with no honey.
and no wings.
sad things really.

GRACE   they sound completely different
from bees.

JEREMY   the birds and the bees.
they're all the same
when you think about what can really hurt you.

GRACE   i don't see it that way.

JEREMY   well, that's the way it is.

GRACE   are you moving in slow-motion?

JEREMY   no. are you?

GRACE   it seems like
you're taking a decade to touch him.
are you scared he'll hurt you?

JEREMY   not at all.
i'm not scared of anything.

GRACE   that must be nice.

a flash of lightning.
thunder rumbles hungrily in the distance.

JEREMY *reaches* BRAHM.
he gently touches him

JEREMY   huh . . .
there are scorpions all over him
huh . . .
does he still have eyes?
interesting. hmm . . .

BRAHM   nothing like skin?

JEREMY   definitely more like touching a cactus.
can you feel that?

BRAHM   not really. you feel something?

JEREMY   almost never.

BRAHM   hmm . . . interesting.

JEREMY   we're high on you right now.

BRAHM   were you low before?

JEREMY   we're high like she was on you!
you're in us right now.

BRAHM   it's going to rain soon.

JEREMY   you can feel that?

BRAHM   been waiting my whole life for it.

JEREMY   it's only rain.
just another thing that's been named.
do you remember your name?

BRAHM   i remember rain.
i remember getting wet
in the rain.

JEREMY   i hate that feeling.

BRAHM   there's nothing better.

JEREMY   i hate forgetting an umbrella.
hate wet socks.
or wet shirts that cling to you.
soggy shoes.

BRAHM   i've waited my whole life
for water.

JEREMY   there's better things than that.

BRAHM   like what?

GRACE   like kissing.
like being seen.
like really being seen.

BRAHM   i'm not here to be seen.

JEREMY   and you're not here to kiss either?
are you? but you did.
you kissed her!

GRACE   me or them.
god.
not her.
how long does this last?

JEREMY   what? life?

GRACE   no.

BRAHM   waiting for rain?

GRACE   this high.
when can i come down?

JEREMY   from your tower?

GRACE   what?

JEREMY   can't rush it, rapunzel!
there's no fireman's pole.
no stripper pole
to slide down
to escape.
just gotta wait.

GRACE   but my head feels like it's on fire.

JEREMY   my whole body feels that way.
i feel like a toasted marshmallow.
here. touch my skin.

GRACE   maybe later . . .

JEREMY   c'mon. just my arm.
you should feel my skin sometime too.
we could make a s'more with our bodies.
something sweet. then something wholesome.
nestle into each other like nestlé toll house.

GRACE   maybe later.

JEREMY   how much later?

GRACE   when i feel better.

JEREMY   so you want me to wait forever then?

GRACE   i didn't say that.

JEREMY   when you met him
did your soul feel like it had a sunburn?
has that feeling peeled off you yet?

like snakeskin
like sheer stockings
like lipstick
like sticky clothes
like all of your clothes . . .

GRACE   i don't know!
maybe.
i don't like the way my head feels right now.

JEREMY   then feel mine.

> *he grabs furiously at* GRACE*'s hands and puts them on his*
> *face*

JEREMY   see . . .
real human skin.
a real face.

GRACE   clocks have real faces too.

JEREMY   and arms and hands.
your hands feel smooth.
your legs smooth?

GRACE   chairs have legs.

JEREMY   and so do you.
are yours smooth?

GRACE   not right now.

JEREMY   can i feel them?

GRACE   not right now.
maybe later.

JEREMY   but if you've shaved them.
they're gonna be
prickly later.

GRACE   does that matter?

JEREMY   it'll feel like touching him again.

GRACE   and what's wrong with that?

JEREMY   nothing.
just i've already done that.
that's all.

GRACE   ok.

JEREMY   ok.

BRAHM   it's going to rain soon.
can't you feel it?
the air feels like that moment
before you run through a sprinkler.

JEREMY   do you think that
grass feels like he does?

GRACE   i don't know. ask him.

JEREMY   do you think grass feels like you do?!

BRAHM   i don't think . . .

JEREMY   right but—
once you did.
you used to.

BRAHM   i don't know if i ever did.
i was always meant to . . .

GRACE   be like this?

JEREMY   you could've been a lot of other things.
you could've done a lot more than this.
hell, i can be a lot more than who i am!
that's just true. that's facts!

GRACE   in arizona . . .

BRAHM   in the desert.

JEREMY   anywhere.
there's always something else to be.
some new part to unearth.
some new thing to name.
always a new germ!
a new thing that can kill you.

GRACE   so what?
you'd name it after yourself?

JEREMY   the point is i could!

BRAHM   i don't know how grass feels.
i'm glad i don't have to think about it.
this is what i am.

JEREMY   does the lawn mower feel good to them?
or like a guillotine?
does grass want to cover the world like shag carpet?
does it want to shag the world!?

GRACE   be quiet for a second, jeremy.

JEREMY   does grass even know how green it is?
hey! you're lookin' kinda green too.
you gettin' nauseous, grace?
or are you growin' roots somewhere down there?

GRACE   please just be quiet for a second . . .

lightning again

the lullaby music rumbles after like thunder
deep like the guts of the world are hungry for something new

JEREMY   when you met him out here, you kissed

BRAHM   and kissed and kissed and kissed

JEREMY   then somehow
it pulled weeds out of you.

GRACE   no . . .

JEREMY   but it trimmed something away!
it clearly nourished something in you.

he kisses GRACE.
he pulls away.

he kisses them again.
he pulls away.

JEREMY   nothing?

GRACE   no. it's just— different.

lightning strikes in the distance
the lullaby thunder rumbles again

JEREMY   what do you want?
what more do you want?

GRACE   i can't—name it.

JEREMY   you could try.

GRACE   i have been.
i've been trying my whole life.
really.

JEREMY   you could tell me.

GRACE   no. don't think i can.
i don't think i can tell . . . you.

JEREMY   well . . .
i think—
one of the scorpions stung me.
possibly hundreds of thousands of them!
and maybe it's best
that i go to the hospital
now . . .

GRACE   but you said before—

JEREMY   i know what i said.
i say a lot of things!
know a lot of things too!
google's in my pocket all the time
and that's not all i keep in my pants!

GRACE   jesus christ.
they're just the family jewels.
it's not the fucking hope diamond, jeremy!

JEREMY   could be!
but you'll never know, will you?
i heard what you said
and now i'm going to the hospital
because i'm just going to the hospital, ok?

GRACE   ok.

JEREMY   ok.

>*he adjusts his clothes*

>*then sets off like columbus*
>*ready to find the new world or a manatee*

GRACE   i feel like throwing up.

BRAHM   it's ok.
out here
you can do that.

GRACE   i know that.

BRAHM   ok.

GRACE   i am ok, cactus!
you don't think i can be ok?
i can do anything!
i'm a fucking artist!
i'm molding the minds of the future!
i'm mold!
clay too!
paint.
a canvas.
or . . . i'm nothing

i'm nameless i'm broken i'm sweating
i'm here i'm nowhere i'm yours i'm no one's
i'm a catch i'm catching a cold
frigid, barren, a plot of land
an object, a fantasy
am i more than just lyrics?
am i cum?
am i an egg?
am i something?
besides this?
am i pain?
am i just hurt walking around?
looking for a band-aid.
looking for a cure.
looking for . . . you?
you never saw *secret window,* did you?!

> GRACE *stumbles to the edge of this world*
> *retches, then vomits*

> *lightning again*
> *lullaby thunder rumbles above them*
> *then just breathing*
> *regaining equilibrium*

BRAHM   one day, i'd like to see your paintings

GRACE   what? while you still can?

BRAHM   yeah.

> *a phone fished from a pocket.*

> GRACE *approaches. wobbly.*
> *holds the screen to what remains of* BRAHM'*s face*
> *fingers gently swipe*

BRAHM   they're very beautiful.

GRACE   thank you.

BRAHM   and they don't have names?

GRACE   no.
well, they're self portraits

BRAHM   there's something peaceful about them.

GRACE   thank you. they're watercolors.

BRAHM   oh, water.
that explains it.

GRACE   explains what?

BRAHM   nothing. i like them.
maybe it explains why i like them.
there's something unknowable about them.
like fog.

GRACE   fog is water too.

BRAHM   really?

GRACE   yes, it's like the clouds walking among us.
fog is just a cloud.

BRAHM   and a cloud is water too?

GRACE   yes.

they're quiet.
the phone is put away.

GRACE stares at BRAHM
then looks at the horizon.

it begins to gently rain.
the world slowly starts to become a watercolor painting

GRACE wipes at their eyes.

BRAHM   do you feel that?

GRACE   yes.
it's raining.

BRAHM   your eyes are too.
why?

GRACE   i thought you were safe.
but you're just—

BRAHM   covered in scorpions.

GRACE   no.
i don't think there is a safe thing anywhere.
not even a safe word.
and even though i know how you could hurt me . . .

BRAHM   i have sharp spines.

GRACE   you're like the cracking of
a library book's spine.
my feelings for you have that smell
that ancient smell . . .

BRAHM   pheromones.

GRACE   no.
it's something else.
can i kiss you one more time?
just one more time?

BRAHM   yes.

they lean in and share a final kiss with BRAHM

BRAHM *'s face disappears into the cactus.*
was it ever there?

GRACE *takes a few steps away*
looks at the heavens
looks at their feet.
bends and fights with their shoes
untying, untangling knots

the saplings, ZUCK, HUGH, *and* LENT, *return years later*
with indiscernible melting paintings of their own
drinking beers now

GRACE *throws one shoe off, then another*

LENT   some people can see things better if they squint.

ZUCK   and some people don't see shit, man.
brought a package to this old man's house last week.

HUGH   you're seriously still doing that on foot?

ZUCK   and i took a photo of it
hit the confirmation button.
and that all goes to the cloud.

LENT   congratulations, sir!
your new fleshlight has arrived!

ZUCK   and he said it never made it to his porch.

LENT   never made it, huh?

ZUCK   never arrived he says!

> GRACE*'s hands become shovels*
> *furiously digging at earth*

HUGH   and every day
there are others like him.
even when i deliver things by drone.
they're alone
and just frantically screaming into the void.

LENT   about things they never got—

ZUCK   about things they paid so dearly for—

HUGH   about these lives
they deserve and can't afford—

LENT   it's beyond sick!

HUGH   it is, man. it is.
but lead poisoning is a real bitch
it fucks up their heads.
fucks up their memories.

> GRACE *plants their feet in the ground*
> *facing away. they squat*
> *and scrape the earth back into itself*
> *then they stand*
> *feet and hands hidden from us*

LENT   it's all fucked up.

JEREMY *drips through like paint in water*
in his element again

JEREMY   no, we're so happy to have you.
the kids really need mandarin!
yeah, i do know a few words.
i have duolingo and google.
yeah, i'm learning. i'm growing even, sure.
i know what i'm good at
but maybe you could teach me a few words?
so i can grow some more.
how to order a drink
how to say good night
all the important things to say
before getting under the covers.
yeah, things before bed!
sure, things like prayers!
always had a thing for nuns.

he starts to chuckle
and then goes
as if wiped away like a familiar mistake

in this silent drizzle,
GRACE*'s hands explore.*
they sigh. they exhale.
their head gently rolls skyward.

the boys drink again
they laugh
they drink again

HUGH   you guys hear about florida?

ZUCK   there's probably a hundred million things
written about florida.

LENT   i read something about a crocodile—

HUGH   oh, i know. terrible.

HUGH   eating a child on the shore
and LENT

HUGH   disgusting!

LENT   of some disney resort.

ZUCK   some last resort . . .

LENT   what?

ZUCK   you know
a last resort means . . .

LENT   the last place you'd want to stay?

ZUCK   in a way.
cause it's like the last action you'd take.
the very last.
and you'd only do it after everything else failed.

HUGH   but isn't that just life? things failing?

ZUCK   well, life isn't a resort!
and like . . . isn't a resort . . .
really just another way to re-sort?

LENT   that's fucking stupid.

ZUCK   well, florida is underwater now!
how fucking smart is that?
fucking genius, you are!

LENT   life's been different!
for your dumb family.

ZUCK   why?

LENT   cause you got to go to these places.

HUGH   ok, guys.

LENT   when they really existed.
you met mickey
and minnie
and buzz lightyear
and pocahontas and—

ZUCK   what? quasimodo?
you tired of leading some quasi-life?
isolating yourself like some hunchback?

LENT   shut up! i've given up so much!
my life's only been only about sacrificing things.

ZUCK   whose fault is that?
who made you give anything up except for yourself?
who told you to be a lesser version of yourself?
you did that.
you fucking did that.

LENT   i fucking didn't.

ZUCK   you fucking did.

LENT   no!
i fucking didn't i fucking didn't!!

HUGH   ok!
that's enough.
isn't it?

> LINDA *arrives in the desert with a canteen of water*
> *she sighs*
> *composes herself*

LINDA   had a feeling this would happen.

GRACE   mom?
you're here?

LINDA   i heard there was some magic
happening out here.
wanted to see for myself.
had to see you
in the flesh.
well—
in person.
well—

GRACE   and you see—?

LINDA   yes
i see you.
you're not a mirage, are you?

GRACE   don't think so. i—

LINDA   shh . . .
it's okay, baby.
this isn't the first time our family has
dealt with this.

GRACE   with what?
failure?

LINDA   no.
this isn't failure.
you're growing into yourself.
we all have to grow from our own shit.
our own fertilizer.

GRACE   so then . . .
you wanted to say something else?

LINDA   yes.
about uncle bruce.
your great uncle bruce.

GRACE   the gay one?

LINDA   no, well, we may have told you that
he was gay but—

GRACE   but he wasn't?

LINDA   he was actually like your cactus.
but he became a tree.
he was so obsessed with the giving tree
it was his favorite book.
and one year he told us all at christmas
that he was going to become a spruce.

GRACE   why didn't anyone tell me about this before?

LINDA   it's not the sort of thing you tell kids.
you wouldn't have understood.

GRACE   and none of you did either?

LINDA   don't assume who we were, baby.
your great uncle bruce

fell in love with a man who
planted trees for a living
and that man helped him find a place to put down roots.
but one day my grandfather
my pop-pop
went out and he cut down every spruce.
every single one.

GRACE   why?

LINDA   i don't know.
there's not always a great reason.

GRACE   what was so threatening
about the tree just staying?

LINDA   nothing! i don't know what to say.

GRACE   well, that's a first.

LINDA   i guess some men were meant to be trees
and some men will never understand
cause they think they're only meant to cut things down.

GRACE   but aren't some men are meant to be still?
like rock, like boulders—like soil?

LINDA   maybe.
maybe . . .
can i tell you something else?
and will you promise that you won't judge me?

GRACE   don't know that i can promise that.
i've been judging you my whole life.

LINDA   truthfully
i wish you wouldn't judge yourself so harshly.

i want to tell you that, yeah—
i fucked a lot. fucked things up too. i did.
i was loose and it felt a lot better to me than being tight.
i kissed a lot of men. a lot of women too.
plenty of people were inside me
but never within my soul.
and there was a time when things weren't so pretty for me.
i hear it in your voice sometimes too.
that things have been ugly for you too.
and we don't have to talk about that.
i used to lock myself away from the world.
i used to avoid my own eyes in the mirror.
and i just wanted to say that—
i'm fine today. really.
these things happen
but i'm okay. okay?

GRACE   okay.

LINDA   years ago
i was sitting in a rocking chair at my mother's house
breastfeeding you.
and she said to me, "you're sitting on uncle bruce"

GRACE   oh my god.

LINDA   i looked under my ass
and i saw this beautiful piece of woodworking.
that was him.
i asked my mother about him
and she told me everything she could.
you were there.
you fed from me.
chewed at my tits
til they were bloody.

GRACE   how did—

LINDA   my grandma was sick at the idea of him
just being lumber.
so she made him into art.
into a kind of driftwood.
she made him into a place for dreams to happen.
he was the most beautiful chair, grace.

GRACE   ok.

LINDA   we sat with him together.
you and me.
and it's important that you finally know about him.
i know this doesn't fix anything
but i'm glad i could share this with you.

GRACE   me too. thank you for telling me.

                            LINDA *approaches* GRACE.

                    she extends her water canteen.
            GRACE *drinks from it like a newborn.*

                        LINDA *goes but not far.*

                        it starts to really rain.
                        everyone is drenched.
                                baptized.

                    GRACE*'s hands continue.*
                    the elbows are at work.

GRACE   i've seen *casablanca*
i've seen *when harry met sally*
i've seen *sleeping beauty*
i've seen *pretty woman*
i've seen *fatal attraction*

i've seen *carrie*
i've seen my face
i've seen my own face
i've seen my own hideous fat face
i've seen *funny face*
i've seen *breakfast at tiffany's*
i've seen *beauty and the beast*
i've seen my own ugliness
i've seen *something's gotta give*
i've seen *never been kissed*
i've been kissed
i've seen *cinderella*
i've been cinderella
i've seen my dirty soles and my filthy soul
and left them somewhere else
for someone else to find
i haven't seen *secret window*
i've never seen *secret window*
i've seen cacti
seen trees
seen rocking chairs
i've seen the end of this world
i've seen my own life
i've seen
my own life at a distance
i've seen that
i've seen
i've seen
i've seen
i've
i've
i've
i've

language crumbles and echoes
a cacophony of sound erupts

it's the sound of drones
it's the sound of rain
it's the sound of the friends' theme song
it's the sound of pleasure
it's the sound of christmas carols
it's the sound of rattlesnakes
it's the sound of babies crying
it's the sound of marvin gaye
it's the sound of tornado alarms
it's the sound of trees falling in the woods
when no one is around

then finally
after heaving breaths

it's only the sound of rain
it's only that

flowers spurt from GRACE's back
they bloom

the rain slows
the rain stops

the painting is finished

Lecture Notes in Computer Science 913

Edited by G. Goos, J. Hartmanis and J. van Leeuwen